DANGEROUS JOBS™

POLICE
IN ACTION

Lissette Gonzalez

PowerKiDS press.
New York

Published in 2008 by The Rosen Publishing Group, Inc.
29 East 21st Street, New York, NY 10010

First Edition

Editor: Jennifer Way
Book Design: Greg Tucker
Photo Researcher: Nicole Pristash

Photo Credits: Cover © Bryan Bedder/Getty Images; p. 5 © Robert E. Daemmrich/Getty Images; p. 7 © Stephen Cherin/Getty Images; pp. 9, 11, 17, 19, 21 © Shutterstock.com; p. 13 © Justin Sullivan/Getty Images; p. 15 © David Glick/Getty Images.

Library of Congress Cataloging-in-Publication Data

Gonzalez, Lissette, 1968–
   Police in action / Lissette Gonzalez.
      p. cm. — (Dangerous jobs)
   Includes index.
   ISBN-13: 978-1-4042-3778-0 (library binding)
   ISBN-10: 1-4042-3778-X (library binding)
   1. Police—Juvenile literature. 2. Police—United States—Juvenile literature. I. Title.
   HV7922.G65 2008
   363.2'3—dc22
                                          2006039079

Manufactured in the United States of America

CONTENTS

WORKING IN LAW ENFORCEMENT

Almost any place you go will have a police force. Towns, cities, and states all have police forces. Police officers patrol neighborhoods to **protect** people and **enforce** the law. They also answer calls for help and investigate crimes. "Investigate" means "to look for answers."

Countries may also have a police force. In the United States, this is the Federal Bureau of Investigation, or the FBI.

People who work in law enforcement must deal with many different kinds of problems and dangers. Because of this, there are many different kinds of jobs in law enforcement.

4

This police officer in Austin, Texas, is using a laptop computer. Police use computers to check on up-to-the-minute information, or facts, to help their investigations.

5

POLICE OFFICER TRAINING

Anything might happen to police officers while they are on duty. Sometimes they get hurt or killed. To prepare for a job in law enforcement, people get training at a special school called the police academy.

There are police academies in every state of the United States. At the police academy, people who want to become officers learn about the law and how to stay safe. They also learn how to drive police cars, how to make an arrest, how to fire a gun, and much more. Learning to be a police officer takes many months!

These New York City police have just graduated from the academy. "Graduated" means "finished and passed a school or training course."

PROTECTIVE GEAR

In the United States, most police officers carry guns when they are on duty. They do this to protect themselves and the people they serve. The most common kind of gun they carry is called a **semiautomatic pistol**. It is a powerful gun.

Some police officers who work in dangerous places may wear **bulletproof vests**. These vests can be made of a strong yet light fiber called Kevlar. Other officers wear heavier body armor and helmets. Those who work with bomb squads, for example, often wear **armor** made with steel. Police protective gear is sometimes called **riot** gear.

Police wear riot gear when they are going into very dangerous settings. Besides wearing Kevlar and helmets, they may also carry clear plastic shields for extra protection.

DANGEROUS PATROLS

Most police officers have an area that they patrol. They keep a lookout for people who are in danger and for **suspicious** activities. Police officers patrol neighborhoods both on foot and in their police cars. While on patrol, they get to know the neighborhood and the people who live there.

Some patrols are dangerous. In places where there is a lot of crime, police may have to go after **criminals** who have **weapons**. Officers who patrol the highways also face danger. Many get hurt by speeding cars when they pull drivers over on the road.

10

When they are on patrol on a highway, police officers face danger from car accidents or drivers at accident scenes.

DRUG ENFORCEMENT

There are police **units** that do only drug enforcement. Their job is to make sure that everyone in a community follows the drug laws.

Drug enforcement can be dangerous. Sometimes officers need to get to know drug dealers so they can keep track of them and catch them breaking the law. To do this, drug enforcement officers may go undercover. Going undercover means pretending to be someone else. An undercover drug enforcement officer may pretend to be a drug dealer. This way, he or she may investigate a criminal and make an arrest later.

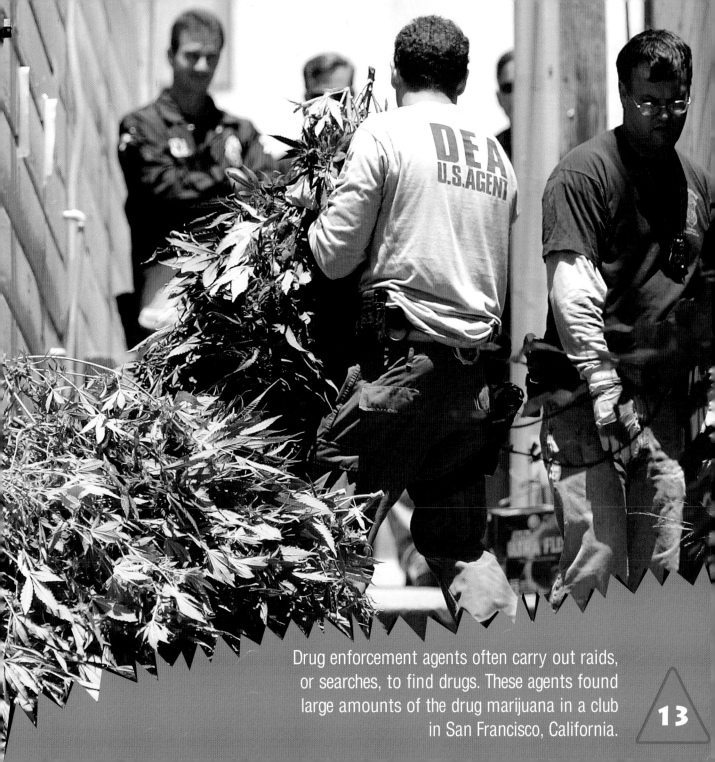

Drug enforcement agents often carry out raids, or searches, to find drugs. These agents found large amounts of the drug marijuana in a club in San Francisco, California.

13

WORKING UNDERCOVER

Not all police who do undercover work are in drug enforcement. Most large-city police forces have detectives who can go undercover. They may go undercover to investigate crimes.

Instead of police uniforms, **detectives** wear everyday clothes to better fit in around people who are not police officers. Because of this, detectives are sometimes called plainclothes police. Wearing clothes that let them fit in helps detectives get close to the criminals they are investigating. Getting close to people who break the law can help undercover police catch a criminal and close a case.

These detectives are dressed in everyday clothes while they are working on a case.

THE SWAT TEAM

Some police departments have SWAT units. SWAT stands for Special Weapons and **Tactics**. SWAT teams can handle dangerous cases in which special skills are needed. They also handle jobs that require more force than a regular officer is trained to use. SWAT teams may get called in to control riots.

Police officers who are in SWAT units carry powerful guns called sniper rifles. They use flashbang grenades or smoke bombs. Flashbang grenades make a loud noise, and smoke bombs let out a thick smoke. These keep people away from areas the SWAT teams are trying to control.

This SWAT team member is ready for action. He is wearing riot gear, a helmet, and is carrying a sniper rifle.

17

WATER POLICE

Water police patrol the waters instead of the streets. They use different kinds of boats to get around on the water. Water police make sure that people who use waterways do so safely. They also enforce the laws of water **traffic**.

Sometimes water police have to do search and rescue work, also called SAR. SAR units are trained to rescue, or save, people from the water. In some cases, police divers go down into the water to search for lost people. Water police need special training because there are dangers when working in and around water, such as drowning.

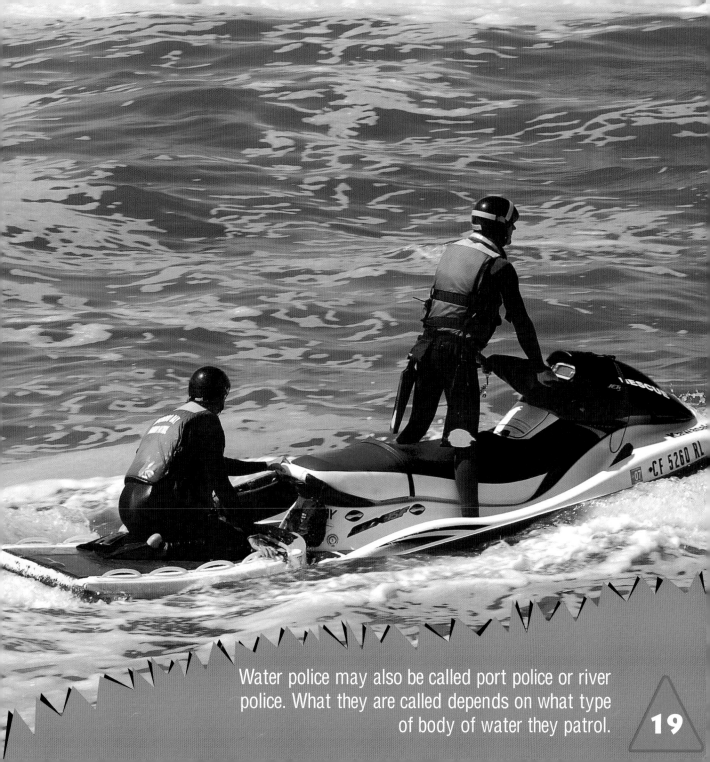

Water police may also be called port police or river police. What they are called depends on what type of body of water they patrol.

DANGERS IN THE LINE OF DUTY

Police officers have one of the most dangerous jobs. According to the U.S. Department of Labor, 18 out of every 100,000 police officers died on the job in 2005. Many of these officers were shot while working their patrols. Police officers also get hurt in car **accidents**. This is because they sometimes have to drive fast. It is harder to stay safe the faster a car is going.

Police work is stressful. Stress is worrying about something. Officers see a lot of scary things in the line of duty. Even the best officer can have a hard time handling a lot of stress.

20

Police officers risk, or face the danger of, being hurt by the people they are trying to arrest. Police must also learn to deal with stress so they can keep doing their jobs well.

TO PROTECT AND SERVE

Even though they have dangerous and stressful jobs, police officers have many reasons for loving what they do. They protect their communities and make them better places in which to live. The people they serve respect their hard work. Police even get to save people's lives!

Police officers often form close friendships with other officers. Most police officers say that they would not want to do any other kind of work. They feel proud living up to the police motto, or saying, "To protect and serve."

GLOSSARY

accidents (AK-seh-dents) Unexpected and sometimes bad events.

armor (AR-mer) A type of uniform used in battle to help keep the body safe.

bulletproof vests (BU-let-proof VESTS) Special chest coverings used to keep people safe.

criminals (KRIH-mih-nulz) People who have broken the law.

detectives (dih-TEK-tivz) People who find out the facts and figure out who did crimes.

enforce (en-FORS) To put or keep in force.

marijuana (mer-uh-WAH-nuh) A drug that comes from a plant.

protect (pruh-TEKT) To keep safe.

riot (RY-ut) A group of people that is out of control.

semiautomatic pistol (seh-mee-ah-tuh-MAH-tik PIS-tul) A very powerful gun that can shoot very fast.

suspicious (suh-SPIH-shus) A person who acts as if he or she has done something wrong.

tactics (TAK-tiks) Plans to do something that requires special skills.

traffic (TRA-fik) The cars, airplanes, ships, or people moving along a path.

units (YOO-nets) Groups of police officers.

weapons (WEH-punz) Objects used to hurt or kill.

INDEX

A
accidents, 20
armor, 8
arrest, 6, 12

B
bulletproof vests, 8

C
criminal(s), 10, 12, 14

D
detectives, 14

L
law(s), 4, 12, 14, 18
lookout, 10

N
neighborhoods, 4, 10

R
riot gear, 8

S
semiautomatic pistol, 8

T
traffic, 18

U
units, 12, 16, 18

W
weapons, 10, 16

WEB SITES

Due to the changing nature of Internet links, PowerKids Press has developed an online list of Web sites related to the subject of this book. This site is updated regularly. Please use this link to access the list:
www.powerkidslinks.com/djob/police/

24